A Prisoner

of

Hope

Reverend Augustine Rugutt

Nsemia

First Edition: December 2015
Published by Nsemia Inc. Publishers (www.nsemia.com)
Oakville, Ontario, Canada

Edited By: Matunda Nyanchama
Cover Concept & Illustration: Robert Kambo Maina
Cover Design: Danielle Pitt
Layout: Cyrus Kioko

Note for Librarians:
A cataloguing record for this book is available from Library and Archives Canada

ISBN: 978-1-926906-45-4

Foreword

We need heroes of faith, people who refuse to give up: prisoners of hope hoping beyond hope; people who will stand above the speaking circumstances no matter how negative and hopeless it gets; people who refuse to be controlled by the surrounding earthly environment; people who reject defeat and hold on to faith; people who become prisoners of hope and whore fuse to die.

A Prisoner of Hope Book is a motivational link between struggle and success. The book captures the life of the author's mother, Pauline Cherono Taptulmat Chepkulul, and her battles with childlessness and debilitating sickness. Cherono Taptulmat was a woman of faith. She hoped beyond hope for a better life and in the process became a prisoner of hope. Her life is inspirational to many that have heard her story, especially when told by her son, the author.

Cherono Taptulmat's story is not an everyday story but one that is relevant to all of us children of God. It mostly inspires mothers who have faced similar circumstances as she did. These are women who endure innumerable hardships in bearing and raising their children successfully in the face of insurmountable challenges.

Cherono Taptulmat's life was full of misfortunes, but she refused to 'die' due to her strong faith in God. Cherono Taptulmat was thought to be barren in a society where a woman's childlessness is scorned. She went childless for over six years. It is thought that this long childlessness was due to the power of her "mother's tongue". The mother, when angry with her, used to tell her "may you be barren for six years." It is believed that it was the power of her mother's tongue that surely led to more than six years of Cherono Taptulmat's childlessness.

It is my prayer that parents, teachers, bishops, reverends, pastors, believers and all people in power will always use their tongues to bless and not to curse others. It is advisable to use your tongue for the good of humanity, with understanding and wisdom, guided by the Lord.

Propelled by this spirit of hope, Cherono Taptulmat raised her children well. This is in spite of the many obstacles on her path. In the process, she inculcated in them the same spirit of faith and courage that underlay the essence of her life. Today, they are a living testimony of this faith.

Although she was surrounded by poverty, Cherono Taptulmat never believed in begging. She was a dignified woman full of determination, and humble enough to be silent even in the face of provocation. Her strong will and desire to improve her well-being and become somebody of reconceive future kept her going.

Befallen by sickness, Cherono Taptulmat sat for over fifteen (15) years without walking. She never gave up and despite the challenges of her condition; she was always joyous and full of peace. She used her tongue to bless her children and grandchildren, giving them hope and values of a lifetime. She fought a good fight of faith by spending most of her time in prayer. To all of us that knew and interacted with her, she indeed was a true prisoner of hope, a source of inspiration and a model to emulate!

To all the people going through hardships in life,such as parents struggling to bring up their children, may hope always cheer you. May you be prisoners of hope. In the end, hope pays off with blessings for the hopeful and Godly impact on others' lives.

"For surely there is an end; and your expectation shall not be cut off."- Proverbs 23:18

Bishop Dr. William Tuimising
A Servant of the Lord Jesus Christ
November 2015

Dedication

I dedicate this book to my dear wife, Nancy Chepkoech for a number of reasons. Driven by her love for me and our family, she sacrificed everything (career, material gain and more) for our mother. My wife's sacrifice extends to our children, Faith Chelangat, Mercy Cherotich, Karen Cherono, Nehemiah Rugutt, Salome Chemngetich and Joshua Kiprono.This work is furtherdedicated to all other ladies of faith,blessed with generosity and a fighting spirit; a spirit that inspires them to fight for love and dignity to the end, and more so when they generously live to the credo: love thy neighbour.

About the Author

Bishop Augustine Rugutt is a trained agricultural engineer, a profession which he practised for many years, although he is a Pastor by calling. He served the government of Kenya for thirteen (13) years. In 2006 he left the government job to dedicate his time in the ministry of serving God.

He is a husband to Nancy Rugutt and father to Faith Chelangat, Mercy Cherotich, Caren Cherono, Nehemiah Rugutt, Salome Chemngetich and Joshua Kiprono. Bishop Rugutt is a spiritual father to many.

He serves God as a full time minister in Jesus Gospel Power Ministries where he is the General Overseer. He is based in Narok Town in Kenya.

TABLE OF CONTENTS

Introduction

"I love the Lord, because He has heard my voice and my supplications. Because He has inclined His ear to me, Therefore will I call upon Him as long as I live." - Psalms: 1-2

A hero of faith is what I saw in my mother. She was a true prisoner of hope and a living testimony for many and all that have faith. Lack of faith makes many people lose hope, which, in turn, leaves them with challenges in continuing to hold on to their vision.

In Life, we often come across and face challenges that make us feel like giving up on our aspirations however noble those aspirations are. It is my prayer that as you read this book, your perspective of life will change and that, no matter the circumstances you encounter, you will always stay strong in faith. Always remember that it is not about you, but about God. When you have faith in Him then hope is assured and so is eventual victory.

I speak from personal experience as I watched my mother's agony, her struggles and eventual triumph. Even in the face of the worst imaginable darkness, our mother never gave up; she kept hope alive. Moreover, as much as most of her environment was punctuated by perpetual negativity, her perspective stayed positive.

She believed in eventual victory without being distracted by her wanting and debilitating situation. For her, the focus had to be God. He, the Omnipresent and Creator of the Earth, had to have an answer for all that was happening. As such she made God her central concern. She knew that, with God, all things are possible. Furthermore, she believed that as long as God kept her alive and that as long as He

1

gave her breath, she had all the reasons to be hopeful for a better tomorrow. To many of us ordinary beings, she held hope beyond hope.

Truly, I cannot fully capture everything there was about our mother. I have summarized the very important aspects in her life according to my observation for the time I knew her and for the sake of clarity in this writing. I share her story because I am sure many of us, in our lives, have either found themselves in similar circumstances or may encounter them in the future.

I believe this experience will be a blessing to many. This is especially for all women who want to be good mothers in their families. I am hoping that the contents of this book will challenge us all and that we would put our hope in God, even as we become true parents to our children and role models in our communities and greater society.

My mother's life story taught me a lot, especially on the futility of bitterness. Yes, there are many people who are bitter with one aspect or another in life. Bitterness invariably has no gain! I learnt from my mother that it is possible to have joy even when 'passing through fire'.

It is my hope that sharing experiences of how our parents brought us up will touch and help many. I have zeroed in mainly on mother's side since I stayed longer with her than I did with my father.

There is one more reason I am sharing these experiences. I simply could not come to terms with leaving the lessons I learnt from my mother undocumented. Her determination to make a difference, despite the many challenges she faced, encouraged me to write this book. They are lessons that can benefit fellow humanity in our journey of life!

A Tribute to Our Beloved Batiem (Grandmother)

It is only God who fully understands the challenges our family went through all the many years of nursing our mother till she peacefully went to be with the Lord.

To our beloved ma and grandma, we thank God for the gift of a great women like you. You have been a treasure in our lives and we will always remember the days we spent together. We cherish you dearly in our hearts for you touched us in many special ways.

Beloved Batiem, you taught us a lot of virtues and moral values: to be obedient children, to respect other people and to live according to the ways of the Lord. You also imparted on us the value of good and healthy relations, and how to relate with people. From you we learnt how to choose friends and how to make friendships last. You treasured education and the culture of hard work. Invariably, at the start of a new school term you advised us to work very hard so that we can become a blessing to our parents.

Beloved Batiem, you loved us fairly and treated us equally. We never complained while assisting you in any way because we loved you. You used to pray for us each day and we shall never forget the verses you loved in the bible because we memorized each day like Psalms 103, 91, Mathew 24 and many others. We will never forget the songs we sang together like "*kona Jesu muguleldo, kolosun*" (Oh for a heart to praise my God) and "*Riba Eutab Jesu*" (Safe in the arms of Jesus). You were a source of encouragement to us all. We will always respect what you went through in your hardships and your ability to hold yourself with such dignity and pride in all your days.

To our lovely parents and relatives, we respect and treasure you for taking care of Batiem in her life time. Aunty Christine Koech you were there for Batiem, you took care of her even when she was sick. Father Joseph and mother Janet Rugutt you also took part in taking care of her. All the other relatives, thank you because you used to visit her.

Our dear Mother Nancy you sacrificed your job and the joy of earning a salary, so that you take care of Batiem. You did not go to many missions and church meetings with Father because you had to take care of Batiem. Father you also made sure that you provided everything that Batiem needed and you took her to the places she wanted to go, you were always an obedient child to her. May the almighty God opulently bless you. We salute you all for that.

Our beloved Batiem, as you enter your new heavenly home, may you rest in eternal peace. Thank you and fare well.

Yours sincerely
Dear Children and Grandchildren

Mother: Pauline Cherono Taptulmat

"Turn you to the strong hold, you prisoners of hope;Even today do I declare that I will render double to you." Zacharia 9:12.

Cherono Taptulmat Chepkulul was born in the year 1938 in Ngesumin village, Bureti constituency. She was the second born child of her parents. In addition, she had one half-sister and six half-brothers, born after her mother became a widow after giving birth to my mother and her brother Richard Kipkoech Ruto.

In their childhood, my mother and her brother Richard faced a lot of rejection from their step father. This was severe to an extent that the stepfather could forbid my mother's brother from getting enough food to eat. Many were times when, as a young girl, my mother could secretly take food to her brother Richard in the bush. The stepfather, however, was not as bad to my mother as he was to her brother. He knew that one day she will be married off and fetch him a substantial dowry.

The parents engaged mainly in farming. Despite the tension in the family and the stepfather's attitude, he allowed Richard and the others to go to school, but not my mother.

She never got the chance to do formal schooling because her parents, like many other parents of that time, did not support education especially for girls. This is despite the fact that there were some homes where parents encouraged their children (including girls) to go to school. As much as she never protested her parents' perception of education, deep down she knew that it was not up to them to decide for her. As such, throughout her life, she lived with constant regret over her 'failure' to attend school. It is a thirst and yearning that she lived with all her life. All that time, she felt that, had her thirst for school education been quenched, then it would have borne good results and made a positive difference to the kind of life she led.

My mother got married in 1956 to Silanga Arap Chepkulul, my father. In those days, that was the normal age for marriage, unlike these days when girls can remain single into their 30s. My father was a simple, unadorned man who did not care for many things around him. He was laid back and led a life of continual lull.

This made my mother the voice of the homestead. She could instruct us on what to do and my father would restate whatever she said as if it were his original idea. In a way, this was a rare situation. In most homes, and especially in those days, men took a lead on many things. Indeed, to this day, men are expected to be heads of and breadwinners in their families!

Despite these unusual circumstances, my mother remained a submissive wife. This was not her only virtue as both a mother and wife. She was also confident, though obstinate, when circumstances warranted; she was strong-willed, a hopeful fighter, faithful to God, passionate about what she engaged in and joyful about life. She had a rare view of the world that substantially differed from those around her.

I believe that it is because of these virtues that we (her children) are where we are today. She raised us to not only uphold these virtues, but also practice and live by them.

My Mother's Health

"Bless the Lord, O my Soul: and all that is within me, bless His holy name;

Bless the Lord, O my soul, and forget not all His benefits: Who forgives all your iniquities; who heal all your diseases; Who redeems your life from destruction; who crowns you with loving, kindness and tender mercies;

Who satisfies your mouth with good things; so that your mouth is renewed like the eagle's." - Psalms 103: 1-5

Pauline Cherono Taptulmat started ailing in her early years of marriage. I would later learn that I (her second child) was only eight months old when she started complaining of pain in her joints. Her sickness would become chronic over time. And as things worsened, many people (including her) thought that she would die soon.

In my early years, I grew up watching my mother suffer in sickness. Anytime I observed her, she wore a resigned acceptance of her condition. She appeared worry-filled to the core. And she had a reason to worry.

At my age of eight months and with her ailing, she must have worried about my upbringing. Who would take care of me were she to die? At the time, my older sister was just four years old; she was not old enough to take care of me, the baby.

As fate would have it, circumstances turned for the better. Our mother survived after two years of serious sickness and God blessed her with two more children. During those two years her half-sister usually came in to assist us. Actually, my mother's half-sister Marceline Kosgei stayed with us until she looked like she was a member of our family; our first born. Indeed, even us children thought that she was our eldest sister.

My father did the best he could have done to see to it that his wife was healed. In fact, he went as far as consulting witch doctors. It was where he knew he could possibly get help but it may also have been a sign of his desperation.

My brother Joseph and sister Chepngeno are two children that our mother was blessed with after her condition improved. Unfortunately, this younger sister passed on at three years of age. She had been diagnosed with an abnormal brain growth.

For our parents, it was not an easy task raising us. As children, we had to adapt to the frustrating life that was characterized by mother's sickness and our family's material poverty. These were big challenges, especially for our mother, given how much work women do around the home. And despite all the trouble, mother worked hard to provide for us. She never allowed her ill health to get in the way of her role as a mother, which included providing us with the simplest of basic needs.

Mother tried her luck in a number of small businesses. She sold maize and eggs, and even brewed chang'aa, if only to ensure we were provided for. Her brewing and selling chang'aa did not last long, however. A neighbor died out of too much consumption. This act dissuaded her from continued production, perhaps viewing it as a cursed trade.

Due to the growing poverty in Koitabai village (our home in Bureti then), mother decided to follow her parents back to Bomet in search of a better life. In part, it was to have access to bigger land for cultivation. In her wisdom, she persuaded our father to sell our ancestral land and have the entire family move to Bomet. He accepted and the entire family moved as planned. This was around 1968. I was three years old then.

In Bomet, my parents bought a bigger piece of land. It was half forested and they did a lot to clear it. Mother could brew chang'aa for people around the area to come and help with the clearing of the land. During this period, her sickness was on and off. She was always complaining of pain in her joints. Without hospitals in the place, she largely depended on herbal treatment.

Despite all and great efforts, our life of frustration did not end with our relocation to Bomet. This situation was compounded by our father's conduct. He would come home drank and would chase mother away. He did not appear to appreciate the gravity of his actions on us as children let alone the impact on our mother given her sickness.

Your guess is as good as mine: his conduct, perhaps made mother's illness worse. However, as she always did, it is not something she would show to us children. She bravely soldiered on.

And no! The end of her sickness was not in sight. The illness persisted.

Our grandparents (Arap Mugenik) helped her get all sorts of medical help, which ranged from normal dispensaries (there were not many hospitals then) to traditional medicine, including visiting witch doctors. The herbal medicines prescribed to her by traditional medicine men and witch doctors were given in varying forms, including direct application through incisions on the skin. This ended up disfiguring her skin extensively as the result of them any scars left by the healed incisions. Throughout her life, the scars served as a constant reminder of the pain she was enduring.

Despite all the efforts made towards treating mother's illness, none of the medicines gave her ailment any promising long term solution. She could get temporary relief but without being cured, for a cure is what she truly needed.

Mother was not the only victim of chronic sickness in our family; father was a sick ling too. Our parents' health issues were on and off for a long time. In the case of our father, he used to complain of stomach problems and often times used herbs for his condition. Some thought it was related to his drinking. He would later on, around 1978, stop drinking but got no reprieve! He later passed on, 1st of August 1982.

What kept us strong, though, was the fact that mother never gave up. In spite of her sickness, she stayed optimistic and hopeful that one day she will be fine.

A Spirit of Determination

After father's demise, mother became the bread winner for all the four us, the three children in the family as well as herself. Poverty continually knocked at our door and was a constant reminder of our unfortunate material condition. However, mother was determined not to let it become our destiny! She resented poverty with every last energy she could spare from her illness. She pulled on all strings within her reach to make sure that we never missed a meal and thus ensured that we had no excuse not to be hopeful.

Just like food, concern for our education became central to mother's focus. She made it mandatory undertaking to assure that our schooling could be achieved. She wanted us to be well educated as a means of securing our future and that of our children. Indeed, she constantly encouraged us on the path of schooling, promising that one day we would be just like other financially stable people.

As she struggled to educate us, she would also make what we perceived as a momentous decision, disposing off a part of our property to enable us pay school fees. She went ahead and sold an acre of land to our neighbor,Arap Kilele, fourteen thousand shillings (Kshs 10,000), which she used the money to cater for my school fees.

I was in form three at the time,this was in 1983 and the money helped me complete school with no major fees problem. Even then, I finished my form four with arrears of four thousand shillings (Kshs 4,000). As much as the debt was a concern, the most important thing was that I could now go to university!

Thank God that university education was paid by the government at the time. Indeed, aside from government paying our fees, each of us got five thousand four hundred shillings (Kshs 5,400) per semester, money that we termed as "the boom". This was money that was meant for our books and clothing, and drawn from the student loans we signed for. For me, this money was not only a blessing, but also my brother's because I used part of it to pay his school fees.

God was faithful to me all through my university study. I experienced no major challenges whatsoever except that sometimes having enough pocket money was an issue.

I finally graduated in 1990 and promptly got a job. Out of my earning, I made savings. I went back to my high school and paid off the balance I owed, as I took my secondary certificates and that had been retained because of the debt I owed.

Mother's commitment to our well-being gave me a perspective in life that I treasure and live with to date. I saw my mother as a sacrificial spirit, and one that laid down everything for her family: to feed us, take us to school, teach us attributes, be our mother and 'father' at the same time. In my view, she worked beyond society's expectations of a woman, carrying out duties of the man and women of the home. She was more than a man of the home. Never did she allow us to be stranded in any situation. She always came up with ideas, solutions and strategies.

As I have alluded to before, when I was almost dropping out of school due to school fees she suggested we sell one acre of land to meet school fees expenses. It worked! I was able to continue with education and finally graduate from university.

I also remember the time my plans for marriage were underway soon after I completed my university studies. Mother advised that we request a relative to give us a lactating cow so that we pay dowry to my parents in-law. This is a cow that I would repay later to the relative. Luckily, the relative agreed and our plans proceeded as intended. I would later make good on my promise and refund the cow to our relative. Once more, mother's idea had enabled us to find a solution that worked for us: we were married and had satisfied in-laws. She was a saviour for the occasion.

As she did all these things, she demonstrated love and devotion of an unmatched degree. She became my role model and source of inspiration. I could not afford to let her down as such I worked so hard in school to give her the life she deserved and dreamt of.

Mother's determination was rewarded. She reaped the hard work she sowed because twenty years later, we were speaking a different language that was not poverty. With our improved material means, we sought to make her comfortable; we took care of her with a lot of affection and spoilt her with love.

Our Mother's Childlessness

"And when Rachel saw that she bore Jacob no children, Rachel envied her sister, and said to Jacob, Give me children, or else I die." - Genesis 30:1

Whenever my mother made her mother angry, grandmother could spit at her saying is *onkenyisiek loo*(may you be barren for six years). This, grandmother said openly! What a curse from a parent? What insensitivity from one's mother, even in the presence of her grandchildren and neighours!

Looking back now, I am baffled as to why grandmother behaved that way! And indeed, for the world most people know, mothers are always seeking to have grandchildren. What kind of woman was our grandmother to wish herself not to have grandchildren now that she was wishing barrenness on mother.

The power of grandmother's tongue was strong. To date, I believe it is grandmother's tongue that rendered mother childless for all those years she sought to have children but did not. In our community, like many African communities, barrenness is seen by many as a curse. In our society, marriage is seen to have fulfilled its purpose when children come. It is always aggravating when a lady does not receive the blessings of her womb and bear children while in a marriage. Such a woman would be shunned, spoken of in whispers and be the subject of gossip and derision. In simple terms: barrenness is a curse in the African family!

On her part, a childless woman agonizes continually how things could change in the face of reproach and ridicule, which usually turns to self-condemnation. Many such women blame themselves for failure to mother children, which only compounds such a woman's misery.

As mother struggled to get children for over six years, she experienced the fury of 'hell on earth'. The stress led her, in her own words, to attempt suicide many times. This followed many attempts to conceive and extensive exploration as to how to cure the childlessness, which many people in the community saw as barrenness. She tried a number of avenues, including consulting witch doctors but all to no avail. She literary gave up, according to her narration later in life.

As she would report later, one days he went to the lake ready commit suicide. As she set herself for the act she had mentally rehearsed, she heard a voice saying that her husband would be blamed for no reason. This startled her! She was not prepared for someone to get blamed for no cause of his own. She made up her mind. Suicide was not the solution! It was not the way out!

She turned to go face the situation. And this she did mainly because of the love of her husband and children.

Our parents used to work for white settlers in Solai, Nakuru County believe that it was for the Grace of God that the old man (father) did not choose to marry a second wife as many would be tempted to do when faced with similar circumstances. In those days, any case of childlessness was blamed on the woman and not on her husband. Most men would proceed to get a second wife who would bear them children. However, father did not get to that point, thank God!

The childlessness planted bitterness in mother's heart. It stressed her and this, I believe,only made her sickness worse. Indeed, it may have been the root cause of the severity of her sickness, including rheumatoid arthritis, which rendered her an infirm till she passed away.

The Bible tells us not to let bitterness spring up out of one. Mother was bitter with life. She was bitter herself and most people around her. She saw life as meaningless in the face of her childlessness. As her bitterness worsened her condition, her sickness became an extreme infirmity in her till she died. It was not easy for her to carry that burden of pain. The weariness in her heart converted into a bile energy that was not healthy for her.

She never lost hope, though. Over the years and after lengthy suffering, she finally overcame her bitterness, and cleansed the bile of energy that weighed her down. Eventually, with restored faith, she was blessed and her womb bore fruit: two sons and a daughter. One son turned out to become a bishop. The devil was after destroying divine destiny, which was in the womb of this lady.

As the Bible says in Proverbs 17:22, "a merry heart works like medicine, but a broken spirit dries the bones".

I believe that during her lengthy childlessness, all her bones were 'dried up' by the sadness and bitterness in her heart. At the time, she had already started complaining of joint pains, which became a challenge over her lifetime. Despite these challenges, her strong will and desire to be somebody in future kept her going. When I was a young man, I could see her using herbs and many herbalists came to treat her. My mother, in her desire to get children did whatever was within her means to get a breakthrough. It never worked. I believe the hand of God was upon her life even in the face of this apparent ignorance.

And once she turned to God, He cleansed her of bitterness. She became truly hopeful and God finally heard her prayers!

The Nursing of My Mother

By now you know that mother's health was consumed by a spirit of bitterness even as she soldiered on in life. From 1996, she endured pain and suffering continuously, this is when the problem of arthritis had intensified causing her to be incapacitated. It was heart-wrenching to watch her in that condition!

As her child, I was moved by her stamina in the face of the suffering. She loved us with all her heart and did all she could for us. Mother had a strong determination to see her children succeed in life.

I was in form two when my father passed away. That was 1982. This presented our family with further challenges, aggravating an already dire situation. Now my mother had to face the challenge of raising us all by herself;the sole breadwinner. But she never gave up.

Meanwhile, my sister Christine Koech was already entangled in wearisome marriage; a pitiable marital union that was awfully frustrating. It reached a point that her husband sent her away for good. My sister, having no other option, came back home to live with us. Here, she stayed for seven years. Following the death of her husband in August 1993, she went back to her home. A widow!

In my view, the seven years was God's way of dealing with my sister's challenges and offering a solution. The alternative could have easily been death. During those seven years, the husband married another woman who died soon after he did. God does indeed work miracles! My sister's departure to live with us may have spared her life!

When I was in the university, I could come and teach in Kiplokyi Secondary School in Bomet County. This was during the long holidays. It is where I met my dear wife Nancy.

I remember the first day in that school, that was in 1987. I entered the form three class to teach mathematics. The class was full. There was a young female student sitting at the back of the class with others. As I introduced myself, it is like my eyes were opened for the first time and then I saw Nancy. There and then I heard a voice saying 'that is your wife'. I was overly mystified as I could not understand what I had heard! It was even more strange considering that it was the first lesson I was teaching in that school. It is like the hand of God had slowly guided me and gently landed me in that classroom on the material day!

I cannot really explain the events that took place afterwards but by the grace of God we got married in 21st December 1990 in Mogoiywet Africa Gospel Church. Our wedding was officiated by the late Rev Johana Chesimet. We were blessed! I felt vindicated that, indeed, it was the voice of God that I heard on that first day in that school.

During our courtship,Nancy was working at Tenwek Mission Hospital. When she visited my home, I told her of my mother's illness of physical weakness and perpetual joint problems. I explained to my future wife that it was my wish that one of us would forego their job to take care of mother.

My position was borne out of the reality and love for our mother. I knew how much she had struggled and continued struggling for us. I wanted to be a blessing to her at all possible costs.

Even as I made the proposal, I feared that my fiancée might say no in which case it would fall upon me to forego my job to take care of our mother. I also did worry that, were I to be the one to forego my job, it would be a challenge for the family. This is putting into consideration society's ideologies and beliefs that a man should be the breadwinner in a family and not the other way around. Would my fiancée agree to this proposition? I worried.

My fiancée after a lot of discussions finally agreed to resign from her job at Tenwek Mission Hospital just before our marriage to take care of mother. It was a tall order I had sought and a major sacrifice on my fiancée's part. This is especially so considering that, at that time, I was still teaching at Ndarawetta Girls Secondary School. This was on a salary of two thousand shillings per month under arrangement with the Board of Management of the school. It was money that could not meet our needs!

This action by my soon-to-be wife was a major blessing that lasts to date!

On my part, I had no other option but to be a blessing to my mother and family. By the Grace of God, I had started preaching by then and believing that God had architectural great future for us all. Life was never easy and we never expected it to be any easier in the future. What mattered most was that mother had a helping hand and one more shoulder to lean on in the face of her troubles. I remember always telling my wife that the problems would end soon. It was never easy for her to comprehend.

"And Moses said to the people, fear you not stand still, and see the salvation of the Lord, which He will show to

> *you today: for the Egyptians whom you have seen today,*
> *you shall see them again no more forever." - Exodus 14:13*

My wife became a nurse to my mother and the training she had received at Tenwek Mission Hospital became of good use for all they ears she devoted to mother's care.

When I look at the sequence of events, God must have led my wife to Tenwek Mission Hospital to be prepared for a lifetime of nursing her mother in-law. I can testify that my wife genuinely sacrificed all for my mother and me. I am forever indebted to her. In fact, God gave her sufficient grace to nurse mother even at the time when mother was fully incapacitated. This lasted over twenty years. Our children have grown up with a grandmother who needed full assistance in all areas of life. I believe the lessons they took, from observing a life of infirmity as my mother's, have made them better prepared to face their own challenges.

What amazes me is that I never saw my wife or children complain of the work they did in attending to mother in her condition. They loved her sincerely and sacrificed all for her sake. This sentiment was summarized in the tribute read by our second daughter Mercy, on behalf of others during mother's burial on 11th October 2014. I believe they derived joy in serving mother since she used to talk well and bless her children and grandchildren.

In her immobile state, mother spent most of her time in prayer and singing hymns to the Lord. I challenge all and sundry to always love people even at their worst conditions. Specifically, I challenge married women to be sacrificial in their lives and love their mothers in-law irrespective of circumstances.

In fact, marriage by itself is a sacrifice, whereby a woman sacrifices her maternal family and cleaves to her husband's family.

"Therefore shall a man leave his father and his mother, and shall cling to his wife: and they shall be one flesh."-Genesis 2:24

Sometimes I ask myself what could have happened if I had married someone else who would not accept the sacrifices that my wife made. Indeed, I ask myself what I could have done had my wife refused to sacrifice her job to take care of mother. It is a tough matter to ponder.

There are families who are now perturbed because their wives have refused to cooperate, especially in supporting their husbands' kin. This is especially pronounced with respect to sons' wives and their mothers in-law.

I will forever salute my wife for her act of selflessness. She is a true wife and one who understands that blessings are provoked. I believe mother blessed us and will never inherit a curse; curses do not come without cause! (Proverbs 26:2.) We all know in our family that we did the best we could and did so till the last minute of mother's life. I cannot forget what mother told me in the last moments of her life, "My son, what else could you have done? Let God do His will."

My Brother and His wife

While I was at the university, it fell upon my brother Joseph to take care of mother. This resulted in my brother not being able to pursue higher education to the extent he and the rest of us in the family would have liked. Most of the time he had to be with mother, a situation that led him to be on and off school.

Due to that challenge, he went up to form four (then termed O-Levels) with his education. I believe he could have performed better than he did were it not for the fact that most of the time he missed school to attend to mother. He is now a farmer in the village where we were brought up, blessed with a family and doing well.

As a family, we are grateful for his sacrifices!

When Joseph later married, it fell upon his wife to help with mother's care. This gave my wife some relief as Joseph's wife took over most of the work that my wife had been doing taking care of mother. Joseph's wife remains a blessing to our family.

*****

With time, we had to take mother to Narok, (where by God's grace we have established the headquarter of Jesus Gospel Power Ministries) where she stayed till she peacefully rested in the hands of Jesus on 3rd Oct 2014 by 3:00p.m.

We consider ourselves to have been fully blessed by our mother. This, I believe, happened because we took deliberate steps to take care of her. Many people have missed blessings from their parents by failing to take care of them. They later on reap curses when they could have reaped blessings. Those who have parents, irrespective of their conditions take care of them, do your best and indeed you will be blessed.

Do not miss your parents' blessings by taking things for granted. We all have across to carry and thus carry your cross well. The Bible says in

> *"Be not deceived; God is not mocked; for whatsoever a man sows that shall he also reap." - Galatians 6:7*
>
> *"Children obey your parents in the Lord for this is right, honour your father and mother ,(which is the first commandment with promise;) That it may be well with you, and you may live long on the earth."- Ephesians 6:1-3.*

A Prophetic Voice

Pauline Cherono Taptulmat was sharp-minded, intelligent and astute. Although the debilitating disease weakened her, making her physically weak, she remained mentally and spiritually strong. Since the year 2000, she spent a good part of her time praying and singing. She always talked of seeing visions. She dedicated all her Tuesdays to prayer and fasting. She could pray with a lot of zeal.

In addition, she had favorite songs. The songs bring us sweet memories whenever we sing them. In her, I saw a mother full of joy and peace. Sitting in one position for over twenty years is not easy, but she was strong in her spirit. I know that the prayers she offered for us will never die. The Bible says that:

> *"They all died in faith, not having received the promises, but having seen them afar off, and were persuaded of them, and embraced them, and confessed that they were strangers and pilgrims on the earth." - Hebrews 11:13*

Looking back, I believe mother foresaw many things. For instance, she foresaw the wedding of our daughters. She saw great prosperity upon our family and saw our sons and daughters in good spiritual and material conditions.

Mother was ever gentle and I remember a day when she told us that we shall have yet another son called Kiprono. As far as my wife and I were concerned, we had concluded that Nehemiah Kiprotich would be our last child. Then things happened that surprised us all.   In the early part of the year 2013, my wife was diagnosed with malaria and typhoid. Nothing changed in her condition even after taking her prescribed medicines. Little did we know that Kiprono was growing in her and by the Grace of God,Kiprono was born in the midnight of 14th November 2013.

Wow!! Mother's prophecy came to pass. As at the time of writing of this book, our son is two years old while his brother before him is seventeen years.

Mother blessed all our children and when she felt offended she forgave all. My brother and sisters' families were forgiven and blessed too whenever any issues arose. Mother believed in 'letting people free' and living unconditionally. I vividly recall in the last month before she rested, she called me and said *"Tun Okosenge Lagokwok"* (your children will be a blessing to you). They continue to be a blessing and our family feels blessed.

Indeed, we need parents who prophesy to their children. I challenge all the parents to be the prophets of their families. Our mother was our prophet and she never discouraged anyone at any time.

I recall when I wanted to leave the government for full-time ministry;mother encouraged me a lot,adding that's my son you have chosen the right path'. This is one of the many decisions in which I sought her opinion. Indeed, in many decisions I made, I sought her counsel. And she never disappointed as she always gave a wise counsel. She was blessed and sensed many things and hence was a well-placed, blessed counsel.

Mother experienced the move of God in her life. In fact, she mentioned in many ways that she was almost leaving this world. There are many times when she said that she has seen Jesus and also she has seen heaven.

She saw many things and sometimes she could say 'I will not tell you what I have seen', perhaps based on her own assessment of the impact revealing it might have. At other times, she revealed willingly! There are times she could say that she was told to read this or that scripture, and all the scriptures she mentioned gave specific messages.

Mother's prophetic tongue remained true till the end. She always believed and never ceased hoping that one day she will be completely healthy and she will preach to the whole world so that they may come to Jesus.

Thousands attended her burial ceremony. It was a sombre occasion and a time to celebrate the life of a woman (our mother) who had touched many lives; a woman whose life offered many lessons. The ceremony was ably presided over by Bishop William Tuimising. He chose the theme Oh Lord; remember me in your kingdom. It was a moving account that saw many in attendance saved. Even in death, mother was touching the souls of many, guiding them in the path of salvation.

As parents, we are challenged to inspire and shape the good of our children's future. It is a challenge that we should always prophesy good things for our children. This is a lesson we learnt from our mother. Where she felt mishandled by any of her children, she could always pray for forgiveness and blessings for the 'offender'.

Mother loved songs like *Kona Jesu Muguleldo* (Oh for a Heart of Praise my God), *Riba Eutab Jesu* (Safe in the Arms of Jesus), *Jehova nechamanak a chame* (Oh God I love you and I know you love me), *Choruenyo Kiptaiyat Jesu*(what a friend we have in Jesus), *Kosobindet Yetindenyo* (The great physician) "*kaagas koya mamieindo*" (I have found His grace is all complete) and many others from the Kalenjin Hymn book.

Aside from the songs, my mother loved the Bible. She had many favourite verses like the following, which will always remind us of her.

> "*Wherefore come out from among them, and be ye separate, saith the Lord, and touch not unclean thing and I will receive you, And I will be a father unto you and ye shall be my sons and daughters, saith the Lord almighty..*" *–2Corinthians 6:17-18*

"O Give thanks to the Lord; for He is good: because His mercy endures forever." (Psalms 118:1)

"Lord, my heart is not haughty, nor my eyes lofty: neither do I exercise myself in great matters, or in things too high for me. Surely I have behaved and quieted myself, as a child that is weaned of his mother: my soul is even as a weaned child Let Israel hope in the Lord from hereafter and forever" - Psalms 131:1-3

"I love the Lord, because He has heard my voice and my supplications Because He has inclined His ear to me, therefore will I call upon Him as long as I live."
(Psalms 116:1-2)

"And Jesus answered and said unto them, take heed that no man deceive you. For many shall come in my name saying am Christ and shall deceive many."
Mathew 24: 4-5

"Thus says the Lord cursed be the man that trusteth in man, and maketh flesh his arm, and whose heart departeth from the Lord. The heart is deceitful above all things and desperately wicked, who can know it". Jeremiah 17:5,9

Mother's Teachings

Mother had unique wisdom and insight into many things. She could teach with humour. Sometimes she employed parables and other times taught plainly. She frequently repeated the saying "*Ye Ngutin chi ibuch, mebonyemoet,*" which means that when somebody spits on you, just wipe the spit off; it will never produce a wound. It means never revenge in situation regarding anything; always do good; never pay evil with evil. Instead, when faced with evil, always resort to doing good. That way, you will be blessed.

There are many lessons we learnt from our mother. I remember when we were in primary school and the subject of theft came up. She taught us never to steal, not even a pencil. As small as a pencil looked, the act of stealing does not change. She taught us to always be honest and do so in all our dealings. This set standards for us, which are reflected in her values; standards which could not be compromised.

Discipline was part of her teachings. Mother resorted to discipline us whenever we failed to meet her set standards. We could even receive beatings if we messed. I cannot forget the days we could steal sugar for purposes of licking! She could always know that we had stolen the sugar. And then she would ask who did it, which we promptly denied even going to the extent of swearing that we did not do it. She could never be convinced; she could then impart punishment and stretch it even to three consecutive days until we confessed and asked to be forgiven.

Looking back and reflecting on mother's stern discipline, terse regime and zero tolerance on failing to heed standards, I realize the kind of values that she helped us internalize. On my part, these values continue to shape my life. Indeed, mother remained my teacher even after I was promoted to be a Bishop. I still cherish the lessons I learnt from her. Mother believed in the word of God with a lot of stubbornness and always strived to do what the Word of God says.

My joy is that my entire family was infused with her teachings. Indeed, all my daughters and our first born son, through constant contact, received her teachings. I believe they will always cherish those lessons. My dear wife also learnt a lot from mother during the constant contact as she nursed mother. I am persuaded that I will be faithful to teach others the good values we got from her.

Mother and Relationships

Mother nurtured her relationships by always asking for forgiveness and upholding silence in the face of provocation. She liked visiting relatives and showed her generosity in the process. Her number one rule was never visit empty-handed. She showed love to her relatives irrespective of how they perceived her. She challenged us to love our neighbours and never to quarrel or raise unnecessary friction with any of them. She believed in fair treatment of all, irrespective of status. This is a virtue we have learnt in our family and even my children always challenge me on the same.

Mother advised against conflict. She had a particular dislike for cases, especially when they involved the court process; she hated it!. This is a value I have also learnt to appreciate: dislike for conflict and associated wrangling.

Mother's brothers and sister used to come and visit with us. Thereafter, she could provoke us by asking that I take her to visit them. And quite often we did.

Mother passed away just as we were planning to travel to Koitabai(our ancestral village in Bureti) to visit her relatives. Our plans were to make the trip in August 2014. However, due to commitments, I postponed the trip to December 2014. Regrettably, she rested before the planned visit could take place.

Relationships are very important for the well-being of society; they are good for us all with respect to our physical and spiritual health. Personally,I have committed to building and nurturing good relationships. No one in our family will ever blame mother for any shortcomings in regard to good and lasting relationships. Mother gave us the 'playbook' that we are duly following. Bishop. I still cherish you

Mother's Departure

"Mark the perfect man, and behold the upright: for the end of that man is peace." Psalms 37:37

My sister and aunt used to take care of mother in the hospital ward in Narok District Hospital. Her health had been going downhill for a while now. And on that morning, her condition looked tragically helpless. To those of us caring for sustaining her in that condition felt like torture to her.

On the morning of Friday 3rd October 2014 around 9:00a.m.,My sister and aunt suggested we "release her" so that she could "go home". It was a painful thought to consider, something near traumatic! Full of tears in my eyes, I spoke to mother and said "then we are releasing you in peace, go home till we meet again." This was followed by a word of prayer. We all prayed with our eyes full of tears and with love.

It was an experience to behold. Having made the decision,I uttered the words to mother and prayed for a peaceful transition to the netherworld. Once I had done that, I felt like a heavy burden had been rolled off my heart. We stayed vigilant in observing her, even as she drifted away. On the same day, at about 3:00 p.m. our mother rested in the hands of Jesus. Peacefully.

As much as her death was sorrowful, the family felt that we had done the right thing. It was time for her to rest in peace.

*****

Soon, preparations started in earnest for laying mother to her final resting place. It was in the rainy season and in our village it was falling non-stop like the famed El Nino. We prayed that we may have a break in the continuous raining, even if just enough to allow us bury our mother in peace.

Indeed, God is faithful. He didn't disappoint us. The rain stopped in preparation for mother's burial. This allowed for the graveling of the road (courtesy of the County Government of Bomet) leading to our home and her grave side. And indeed, the rain stopped for mother's peaceful burial, where thousands attended and many got saved.

Mother was laid to rest on Sunday 12th of October, 2014. It started falling again soon after the burial. God had heard our prayers.

*****

Death is a mystery but what is comforting is that mother rested in the hands of Jesus. She always prayed for the development and peace of our land. I strongly believe that her prayers were answered and we continue to enjoy peace in this great land. Our mother left her family in peace after showering blessings on all of us: her children, grandchildren and future generations in the lineage.

Mother also had some parting instructions to us all. She cautioned that no one should sell the land of Arap Chepkulul (my late father) for it is inheritance to us, our children and our children's children.

We are indebted to her in many ways and we shall always miss her wise counselling and love. I am persuaded in my heart that when we reach heaven then we shall be together and glorify God. I challenge you to always put your faith in God, for one day God will wipe your tears away.

"And God shall wipe away all tears from their eyes;and there shall be no more death, neither sorrow,nor crying, neither shall there be any more pain: for the former things are passed away." - Revelation 21:4

The Value of a Parent

A parent is a pillar in a family without which the family would fall. A parent is a magnet to the family around which the family gravitates and without it the family would scatter wide.

Aside from providing food, shelter and clothing for the children, a parent does more. The parent gives vision to the offspring and inculcates values in the children. These values form the foundation of the children's lives and hence determines their success later in life.

Today, we watch situations where parents are hardly engaged in the lives of their children. It is unfortunate that these parents miss the chance to enjoy the lives of their children as they grow up. In addition, they miss the opportunity to give directions to their children before it is too late.

Today, there are many children that were never moulded by their parents and surely missed great opportunities and blessings. Positive values moulded at family level and imparted early in children's lives, are the basis of a strong community foundation.

Parents hold the destiny of their children in their hands; they hold the key to their children's future and success. And they can make that future bright if only they engaged properly, meaningfully and did their duty in the spirit of the Lord.

We are a family that counts our blessings for the life of our mother. She was an inspiration, a role model and an advisor in many ways. Personally, I believe she understood my calling and supported my calling to do the work of the Lord.

As indicated previously, when I told her that I was resigning from government for full time ministry, she encouraged me adding that I had chosen the right path.

Parents bring stability to families. Their role, is in part, to provide unity. They are a knot tying the family together. Parents are the source of inspiration, encouragement and blessings. These are essential ingredients for success in life. Indeed, there are many people who would have attained more than they did because of lack of parents' inspiration, encouragement and blessings. Words from a parent are strong and active, and manifest themselves through a child's life.

Children, on the other hand, need to respect and listen to their parents. They need to hear the voices of inspiration, the voice of encouragement and the blessings that come with that. It is important to reciprocate, despite the challenges faced daily. We are always challenged to do the best to our parents so that they may leave us with blessings.

Norms and Values Taught by our Mother

I have come to believe that God has blessed some people with inherent wisdom, much of which manifests itself in the life they lead. And this wisdom will find expression no matter one's level of formal education. This was the case with our mother.

Despite the fact that mother did not pursue formal education, God still empowered her with inborn intelligence. She had great insights into issues and she demonstrated a high level of understanding of many aspects of life. This baffled even some of the most educated people around us. If you read a verse to her once she could not forget it. And more, she accurately laid the context and relevance of the verse as it applied to modern life.

In addition, mother taught us many values. I have highlighted some of these for the benefit of others, and indeed in line with her teachings with respect to generosity.

Generosity: Mother believed in sharing. She believed that whoever enters your home should be given at least a glass of water, that is if there is nothing else to offer. She taught us to always be hospitable and tender to all. And for that the reason, for all we know, the visitor could be an angel or a person in distress in search of a refuge. Both are blessings and we should be generous to them.

Honesty: Mother believed in being humble and trustworthy. She always reminded us never to possess or seek to possess anything that did not belong to us. She taught us not to be covetous of others' possessions. When I was in primary school, she would always tell me not to even take something as small as a pencil, which belonged to somebody else. I believe I live to this teaching for it was captured in my form four leaving certificate. The teachers said that I was honest in my conduct in that school. I attribute this to mother's teachings. It is a character trait I acquired as a young child and as I grew up under her care and tutelage. It is a trait that I continually work hard to pass to my children and those that I interact with from the larger community in which we live.

Forgiveness: Mother believed that you should always forgive people irrespective of how they treat you. As said elsewhere in this book, she had a favorite saying that *"ye ngutin chi ibuch, mebonyemoet"*, meaning that "when someone spits on you then wipe it off, for it will never become a wound". She stood for forgiveness rather than revenge. I believe she understood the futility of revenge for it is likely to cause unnecessary agony and a cycle of revenge, which does not help anyone.

In any misunderstanding with our neighbours,she was always quick to ask for forgiveness. There are times when our neighbours came quarrelling us from across the fence separating our properties. This could happen due to one reason or another. Mother always asked us to be silent and let the person quarrelling be worn down and leave. One of her greatest weapon was silence. Sometimes I wondered how it came to be. It is like mother walked under revelation. Jesus also used silence as a weapon to finish his enemies.

"But Jesus held His peace (remained silent). And the high priest answered and said to Him, I adjure you by the living God, that you tell us whether you be the Christ the Son of God." - Mathew 26:63

I have learnt to always contain myself and be silent irrespective of the level of provocation, a value I treasure to date.

Debts: Though we were not endowed with wealth or much in terms of material resources, mother hated being in debt. She always warned us against getting into debt. I am sure she understood the negative and (possibly) debilitating effects of debt on a person. Living debt free also compels one to live within one's own means. I always work hard to stay without debt, although it is still a challenge to me. I have laid my trust in God to help me overcome the tendency towards indebtedness.

On the other hand, mother counselled us to be patient with people who owed us in case they failed to pay us on time. Over the years, I have found that it is always easy for me to release people when they borrow from me in case they are facing challenges.

I am always trusting that God will answer my prayer for a time when I will be fully debt free.

Hard Work: Mother despised laziness and deplored wasted potential of people that did not appear to work hard enough. She hated poverty and always wanted to see that we move from a low status level to a higher level. And she saw hard work as the means for changing our status. Shew as always keen to know my class position whenever we closed school. On my part, I was inspired by her concern and felt that I should never let her down. Even in her state of near incapacitation, she did the same to our children. She inspired them to always aim higher. Indeed, she could implore them to work hard and get more than one degree, asking them to surpass the extent of higher education I had attained.

Discipline –Mother counselled us to be disciplined. She further insisted on children being disciplined, following rules and living in an orderly manner. She never brooked nonsense or tolerated mediocrity. With respect to her children, she was a true disciplinarian. I got many beatings from her, though my father was not keen in beating us. In fact, there are times he told her to stop beating me. She could not stop beating until you ask for forgiveness and promise that you won't repeat the same mistake.

Love - Mother believed in loving people irrespective of the treatment they gave one. There was a bad incident when my elder sister, Christine had a misunderstanding with her late husband Paul Cheruiyot. I was in third year in the university and mother came to look for me so that we go for dispute resolution in Olenguruone. It was one of those cases I do not like to remember. Mother was abused with all the unprintable words by the son in-law and I was restricted from standing up and hitting the man since it was too much to bear.

What shocked me was that my mother was not moved and she continued saying to him "You are still my son in-law." The case ended unceremoniously. We ended up going home with my sister and she stayed for seven years. She came to resettle after the man passed on. He died young and still mother cried for losing a son in-law. Wow!!

Indeed, she loved people irrespective of their status and that is indeed 'agape' love. True love!

Purity: Mother understood that children could still go astray despite the teachings of their parents. During our schooling days I used to have friends of both genders who would come home to visit us. Mother welcomed them all with a lot of joy and offered great hospitality. What always surprised me was that after they left, it would be her perfect 'teaching moment' for me. This happened especially with respect to the opposite sex. She would say "do you want to marry her? I don't want to struggle for you in vain". In her mind, she was warning me against getting into relationships with girls before I was ready for marriage. She could talk to me with such passion on the subject of remaining upright and pure, something that would make me cry. Indeed, she helped me to stay pure and to pursue righteousness till my marriage.

Although this was harsh, it helped me a lot and prevented me from going astray. Indeed, the Bible admonishes parents to teach their children.

"And these words, which I command you this day, shall be in your heart. And you shall teach them diligently to your children, and shall talk of them when you sit in your house, and when you walk by the way,and when you lie down, and when you rise up. And you shall write them upon the posts of your house, and on your gates." - Deuteronomy 6:6-9

In our generation, we need parents to pay more attention to their children, especially on matters of relationships. Parents need to be concerned with the welfare of their children and in the process impact good norms and values on them. Previously, when I told her that I was resigning from government.

Dying the Death of the Righteous

"Who can count the dust of Jacob and the number of the fourth part of Israel? Let me die the death of the righteous, and let my last end be like his!"- Numbers 23:10

In the above verse, Balaam acknowledged that the dust of Jacob cannot be counted. Indeed, he desired to die the death of the righteous. Surely all people will die one day but it is important to understand that there is the death of the righteous. There is also the death of the wicked. The righteous will sleep in the hands of Jesus as they await the day of resurrection. Indeed, death is different in all aspects. I am a firm believer that all the prisoners of hope will die the death of the righteous whereby their end is peace and in the hands of Jesus.

"Mark the perfect man, and behold the upright: for the end of that man is peace."- Psalms 37:37

The day my mother slept, around 3:00 p.m. on 3rd October 2014, I wrote an SMS to my spiritual father, Bishop William Tuimising. I did the same to my associate pastor Dan Chepyegon and two friends, Josiah Sigei and Samuel Chelule. The message read "Shalom, I have released my mother to go home. I don't want her to suffer again; she has endured enough."At 3:00 p.m.on that day, mother rested peacefully in the hands of Jesus. Although death is a mystery but it is good to die the death of the righteous.

Many graveyards and cemeteries have the writings R.I.P. (rest in peace) but the challenge is that most of the people we are wishing to rest in peace were never in peace while alive. If indeed we want our dear ones to rest in peace, then let us teach them the path of righteousness and also live our lives in righteousness so that one day we will truly rest in peace. The bible says that, precious in the eyes of the Lord is death of His saints.

"Precious in the sight of the Lord is the death of His saints."
- Psalms 116:15

Mother rested in peace and I believe that she died the death of the righteous. As long as she was alive, she was always full of hope. She prayed and sang for the Lord. We cannot erase death but we can decide the kind of death we would like to die. And this can be achieved through our actions, our relationships and the values that govern us in all that. Prisoners of hope know that one day they will die, and they always live in hope and faith till the end knowing they will die a righteous death.

David served God's purposes in his own generation, he fell asleep and was buried with his fathers and his body decayed (Acts 13: 36). I believe that is the kind of death for the righteous, fully serving God's purpose before death.

A Discerning Mother

I cannot forget the reaction of mother when I told her that I was leaving my steady government job to dedicate my time fully to the ministry of serving God. She simply said: "my son you have chosen the right thing."Another mother would have seen it differently.

I must confess that it was not an easy decision to leave the government job where I was serving on permanent and pensionable terms. However, I made it happen in 2006. It was not easy for my relatives and friends either. Most of them, except my mother and other family members, were against my resignation. They believed that it was not a good career move to resign from a steady government job in favour of full time ministry.

Many of my relatives, mostly Christians, could not imagine their son getting out of permanent and pensionable employment in the name of preaching. My uncle one day told me thus: "because you really love God, why don't you give half of your salary and continue in government since your family is still young"?

On the other hand, my wife had accepted the path I had chosen, but she was under great pressure from relatives to convince me to stay in formal government employment.

However, I saw myself serving the government of God where one walks every day by faith. And with the support of my family and my faith in God concerning the ministry, I felt confident with the move I was making.

I believe my mother reflected on the journey we had travelled and, with faith, felt confident in supporting me. I recall that her life changed substantially for the better after

I got full time employed with the government soon after my graduation from university. Unlike earlier days, mother could get whatever she needed, a commitment I had made to ensure.

However, she encouraged my move to join the ministry full time. I believe that her faith underlined this support. She knew that God will not frustrate us when I got into serving His people full time. It was a higher and greater calling!

It is my conviction that we should pray to God to give us discerning parents or mothers. Discerning parents will not mislead their children. If my mother had told me not to leave the government, because of my love for her, I would have followed her advice and hence missed out in doing the will of God.

How many mothers have possibly misled their children? Indeed, we need discerning mothers who are quick to discern the will of God and give clear directions to their children.

May God raise mothers in the land of Prisoners of Hope. Let God fill them with the spirit of discernment so that their families will be in safety. Abigail saved her family from the wrath of David because of her discerning spirit(1 Samuel 25: 23-34).Her husband Nabal could have landed their family into trouble if not for Abigail. I believe my mother had the same spirit as Abigail. By no stretch of imagination am I implying that my father was a fool or useless for that matter. However, I know of many circumstances where the words of my mother brought us out of embarrassing situations as a family.

I intimated earlier on, that my father was a simple man of few complications. He was not bothered with many things, but he loved us a lot. That said, our mother was key to our discipline. She could not tolerate mistakes and ensured that, for each mistake we committed, we duly paid through corresponding punishment and remedy. And she disciplined us more (whenever we messed) than our father did. Some of the punishments could include beatings and, often times, it was my father who implored mother to stop the punishment when he thought it was going too far. He could ask her to stop, imploring her not to beat us again.

My brother did not face as intense motherly discipline as my older sister and I got, something I wish could have happened. And this is because by the time he was growing up, mother's health, and hence her strength, had started deteriorating and she could not assert herself to the degree she did with us.

Parents, and especially mothers, should arise and firmly take their position in the family. A family with a discerning mother will go much farther than in the case where a mother fails. Indeed, I believe that where the mother fails to discern things and act accordingly then there is always confusion.

Refusing to Die

Death stared at mother many times and, whenever this happened, it worried us. We worried that we could lose our loved one and that we would miss not only her wise counsel but also the spiritual presence that was part of her being. However, mother simply refused to die, cheating death at every turn.

As a God-fearing people, we attributed this to her place in the face of the Lord, and the Lord's place in her being. It is possible to die earlier than the appointed time of God. However, prisoners of hope like our mother, refuse to die since they are always looking forward to better times to come. They are carried by hope, which allows them to face even the worst of circumstances.

Mother always held up to faith. She believed that one day she will be well. Her sunset days were always joyous and peaceful, and especially when surrounded and comforted by the appropriate care from her children and grandchildren. We are confident that she enjoyed life to its fullness.

It does not matter the circumstances one is facing in life. It is always good to refuse to give up. Never ever give up hope! Soldier on in faith! The Bible says that:

"By faith Moses, when he was come to years, refused to be called son of Pharaoh's daughter: Choosing rather to suffer affliction with the people of God, than to enjoy pleasures of sin for a season." - Hebrews 11:24-25

And that is what made the difference in the life of Moses. He preferred to suffer than to enjoy pleasure that would be short-lived. Indeed, the wilderness experience was not easy, but God was with him. As children of God, refuse to live below the God-ordained standard. Refuse to die before fulfilling your mission on earth. Refuse to die so that you can touch the lives of many others and occasion their salvation!

I believe that mother fully lived and fulfilled her life's mission on earth. She lived to see our son Joshua Kirpono whose birth she has prophesied. This was a time we thought we had closed the chapter of getting more children. Joshua was born fifteen years after the one he follows. Following Joshua's birth, mother embraced him in a scene similar to the biblical incident where Simon, on seeing Jesus, passionately embraced Him and said your servant can go now for He had seen the salvation of Israel.

The Bible says when we love God, He will satisfy us with a long life and hence we should refuse to die in order to be satisfied with the long life; we must refuse to die before we fulfil our mission on earth.

"Because he has set his love upon me, therefore will I deliver him;I will set him on high, because he has known my name. With long life will I satisfy him and show him my salvation"- Psalms 91:14,16

The Power of a Praying Mother

"Oh thou that heareth prayer unto thee shall all flesh come ". Psalms 65:2

Indeed, God hears our prayers. Mother prayed for many years and reserved Tuesdays for prayer and fasting. Due to prayer, she got major relief from the debilitating effects of the disease. This is how the effects of rheumatoid arthritis, which had already deformed her body, subsided for a while. For over twenty years, mother never got any other sickness other than what she was suffering from. It is only just before she passed away that she got some complications, perhaps associated with her inactivity. Many a times she could talk of seeing visions of Jesus and heaven. Few of us could believe her visions but I knew that she was always in communication with God. She talked about heaven with a lot of joy and longing.

One day, I came into the house and she said that, when I entered, she saw a shining light. This is not easy to explain. One day she said "wow, I am seeing our home full of blood!! There is flow everywhere in this home; we are covered by blood of Jesus."

Prayerful people are full of joy, mother was always joyous in her life and there is no one time that she looked disappointed. I believe the prayers she prayed will never die. She has indeed gone to be with the Lord since, the prayers she prayed will forever live and come to reality. She could pray fervent prayers until she starts sweating.

Where is a praying parent? Many children could have gone far in life if only they had prayerful parents. Always pray for your offspring and desire good for them. I am glad that the prayers of my mother will go beyond my life to our offspring, for she saw and prayed for them all. In fact, she saw the weddings and the wealth of our children and we are waiting for the same at the appropriate time.

We need prisoners of hope in our generation. There are more people who are hopeless than those full of hope. Let us give hope to our generation through our prayers and sharing.

Let your children listen to a voice of hope crying to God. We need parents who give hope to their children even during hopeless situations. I heard mother always mention all her children and even the grandchildren in her prayers. Thanks be to God that she prayed for at least one year for Joshua Kiprono. He is now almost two years as I write this book. Although he may not remember his grandmother, he is a product of her prayers.

Mother could see many visions of which we are not able to document. Most of the mornings, she could wake up and speak of what she saw. I wish we could write it all down to share with our wider society. One morning she said "wow! Heaven is very beautiful." Other times, she could say one thing and refuse to elaborate for reasons best well known to her.

"But we are not of them who draw back to perdition: but of them that believe to the saving of the soul." - Hebrews10:39

Mother turned her adversary into a blessing by always praying with zeal. She took most of her time in prayers, interceding for her family members, relatives, neighbours, leaders and the country at large. She could ask for the names of leaders and the next time you could hear her praying for them. Her prayers moved her to a level where she started seeing visions and, many a time, talked of what she was seeing but how many people believe in visions? How I wish we recorded all she saw and told us!!

I can recall the many times I went home (when she was staying in the village at Ndarawetta) and as soon as I arrived, she could say that she had seen me in the morning and hence she knew I would be home on that day.

A Thorn in the Flesh

"And lest I should be exalted above measure through the abundance of the revelations, there was given to me athorn in the flesh, the messenger of Satan to buffet me, lest I should be exalted above measure. For this thing I be sought the Lord thrice, that it might depart from me."
-2 Corinthians 12:7-8

And lest I should be exalted above measure through the abundance of the revelations,there was fire to me, a thorn in the flesh, and the messenger of Satan to buffet me, lest I should be exalted above measure.

Sometimes you wonder about the dealings of God. Paul prayed thrice concerning the thorn and God told him that His grace is sufficient. I have come to a realization that many families in this world have "a thorn in the flesh". The challenge is what do you do when the thorn hurts?

Elsewhere, I discussed my wife's acceptance to nurse my mother due to the latter's incapacitation. It was fortuitous and thanks be to God that my wife, before marriage, had undergone training in nursing at Tenwek Mission Hospital. My wife's commitment is underlined by the fact that she willingly resigned from her job before our marriage. This was after I shared with her in-depth information about my mother's condition and the choices we had to address in regard to mother's situation. In short, mother had weakened substantially and needed a constant helping hand.

It is then that we agreed that one of us would stay home for mother's sake. Looking back today, it is obvious that my wife's training as a nurse was God's plan. And she invested this well service to her mother in-law for a period of over twenty years. In those years, we did what any Pentecostal preacher could have done but still our mother was not completely healed.

Over time, we have learned to trust in God in all circumstances no matter the nature of those circumstances. I always marvel at God's kindness and grace, which was bestowed upon my as wife for all those years, leading her to be patient and nurse our mother with diligence and dedication. I believe, to date, that God's hand guided us to marriage and resulted, perhaps, in mother living longer than she may have lived without the attention and care my wife accorded her.

You must have known by now that I had a close attachment to my mother. By extension, I believe that all men have a close attachment to their mothers. This natural bond nurtures relationships and allows for family tranquility and growth.

It is my advice to married women to love their mothers in-law for the sake of peace and harmony in their own homes. In turn, they will win the respect of their beloved husbands while strengthening their families' bond of love. There is always a price to pay in this life,i.e. carrying one's cross. It is like wearing a crown of thorns or a thorn in the flesh! Endure the pain of your thorn in the flesh and the grace of God is sufficient reward. Paul understood the reason why the thorn was in his flesh, but many of us may never realize the reason for enduring similar pain. Whatever the case, always remember that the grace of God will be sufficient reward.

We learnt that it does not matter the kind of a thorn that is in one's flesh. Face it, accept it and endure believing in God for more grace each day and each year. Only put your trust in Him for He will neither fail you nor forsake you.

The joy of the Lord became our strength all those years of nursing our mother. All through we did not waver, for instance, at no one time we wished our mother were dead, indeed, over time, we realized through God's grace, that death is irresistible and indeed our mother went to be with the Lord at His appointed time. Jesus said to His disciples:

"These things I have spoken to you, that in me you might have peace. In the world you shall have tribulation; but be of good cheer I have overcome the world." John 16:33

In the many intervening trying times, the devil could whisper and say "where is your God in this situation?" But our faith and hope in God became stronger each day as we fully understood that God is God no matter what.

I leave you with the same message: that in trying times, remember that God does not change! And that God is God no matter the circumstances or extent of our pain! And that God rewards (and does so abundantly) the sacrifices we make for fellow man.

I am sure that, as you have read this book, you have been challenged to put your faith fully in God. It does not matter if you have a thorn in your flesh, wait on God and again I say wait. Trust in God and you will be stable in all situations.

God bless you.

Eulogy to the late Pauline Cherono Chepkulul

Birth: The late Pauline Cherono Chepkulul was born in 1938 in Ngesumin village, Bureti Constituency in Kericho County. She was the daughter of the late Kipruto Arap Mugenik and the late Taplunguny Mugenik. She was a sister to Richard Rutoh, Simon Rutoh, David Rutoh, the late John Rutoh, Marcelline Koskei, Joseah Rutoh and the late Jonathan Rutoh.

Marriage & Family: The late Pauline Cherono Chepkulul got married to the late Barnabas Kiprugutt Arap Chepkulul of Koitabai Village,Bureti Constituency in Kericho County in 1956. Together they were blessed with three children namely, Christine Koech, Bishop Augustine K. Rugutt (Jesus Gospel Power Ministries, Narok) and Joseph Rugutt. The late Pauline Chepkulul and her family later moved from Koitabai Village in Bureti to Ndaraweta in Bomet County, where they have lived up to date.

Work: The late Pauline was a peasant farmer and also engaged in many small businesses.

Character: The late Pauline Chepkulul had a great desire to see her family come out of a low standard of living to a respectable and stable status. This desire made her to try many small businesses. She further encouraged her children to work hard in school and was committed to see them go to the highest levels of attainment. Pauline went as far as selling a piece of land to cater for school fees for her eldest son, Bishop Rugutt. She was dedicated to her work and family, a virtue she taught and passed on to her children.

The late Pauline was humble, generous, friendly and a good family advisor. She was a role model in many ways. She taught her children to always respect and forgive people and never to revenge in anything. She often repeated the saying *"Ngo ngutin chi, ibuch, mebonyemoet"* (if someone spits on you, just wipe for it's never a wound). She was generous and always taught her children to do the same. She further taught them to love people and if someone owed them anything, to be patient until the person is able to pay the debt.

Christian life: The late Pauline Chepkulul started going to church in the early 1970s, but her life took a drastic change when she was invited to a Christmas party by Stanley Turgut's family in the early 1980s. She got saved in the party and also received a Bible and a Kalenjin song book. Her faith was enhanced by the salvation of her son (now Bishop Rugutt) and she steadily grew in the faith and was always eager to be faithful to God in all her life. Pauline was very devoted in paying her tithe and offering and was also a strong intercessor. From the year 2000, when she became incapacitated till her departure, she unfailingly fasted and prayed.

The late Pauline Chepkulul had a prophetic voice, despite her weak body. One day she told her son (Rev Rugutt) that you will still have another son called Kiprono. She also added that her granddaughter Viola would be married before Pauline's departure from this world. Both events have come to pass. Other prophetic words are yet to be fulfilled. She always prayed for the well-being of her family and the nation at large. The late Pauline's Christian life was such an inspiration and was so strong in her faith that she never wanted anyone to sympathize with her physical condition.

Health: The late Pauline Chepkulul started complaining of joint pains as early as when she was in her 30's. Initially, she used herbal medicine for treatment until early 1990's when her children took her to TenwekMission Hospital for further diagnosis. After many visits to the hospital and medication, she was diagnosed with rheumatoid arthritis. The doctors attending to her said the disease had no cure, but could be managed with consistent medication. The late Pauline became fully incapacitated in the year 2000 when the said disease destroyed her legs and hand ligaments. During the said period, she stopped using or taking any kind of medicine and kept on confessing that "I am believing in God that I'm healed". In the year 2013, she developed other complications upon which the doctor prescribed further medication for her. The late Pauline became seriously sick starting the month of August 2014 and was admitted at Narok Referral hospital where she was treated and discharged. She was later readmitted on 31st September 2014. She remained on oxygen support until her departure on Friday 3rd October 2014 at 3:00 p.m.

The late Pauline Chepkulul leaves behind three (3) children, thirteen (13) grandchildren and five (5) great grandchildren.

Pauline was a great fighter; she fought a great battle and finished well. Mother farewell, you were our role model, intercessor and inspiration.

Rest in the hands of Jesus until we meet again and, with faith, felt confident in supporting me. I recall that her life changed substantially for the better after I got full time

From left Augustine, wife Nancy with the prophetic son Joshua, Faith, Mercy, Caren, Nehemiah, and Salome. They served mother Cherono and Grandmother with a lot of Love.

Testimonials

I always loved to visit the late Mother Pauline Cherono Taptulmat. To me and my wife, she is an enigma of hope. Her life history as described in this book clearly speaks of how we must not reject any one on account of challenges because the future is always a mystery.

She always shared her testimony of God's goodness, requested us to sing a hymn together and to read her memorized scriptures. She always prayed for us and for Bishop Rugutt's ministry and family. Mama casted her anchor on the solid promises of God and never gave up speaking hope, offering fervent prayers and blessing everyone who visited her.

I remember asking myself how was it possible for someone who was unschooled and could not study the Bible on her own rejected Satan's antics to use her challenges and make her question her Sonship in God? How did she understand that her sickness early in life never embarrassed Jesus? That is only possible for one who is baptized by Holy Spirit. Hard times often are Satan's weapons to tempt us abandon God. For Paulin, she trusted in God, was strengthened the more by her unfavorable condition and demonstrated that being a prisoner of hope is steadfastly holding onto God's promises "until He withdraws them" if that was possible.

Dr. Richard Ronoh,
Lecturer, Researcher and Consultant,
Management, Administration and Policy

Bishop Rugutt's mother's, Pauline Taptulmat Chepkulul, was a great mother not only to her childen but also others that had a chance to interact with her.

Despite her poor health, she was always positive. Anyone meeting her for the first time would not know she had a problem. She would smile, talk positively about life and encourage one with words of hope for a better future. This is in contrast with many people in her state who would only be complaining about their condition and suffering.

Pauline Chepkulul inspired us all, her children and grandchildren to great spiritual, academic and professional heights. Indeed, she was a prisoner of hope and offered great lessons for us all.

Joseah K. Sigei
Principal, Ngito Secondary School
Narok County.

www.ingramcontent.com/pod-product-compliance
Lightning Source LLC
Chambersburg PA
CBHW032052040426
42449CB00007B/1080